Manny Ramirez

and the BOSTON RED SOX

2004 WORLD SERIES

by Michael Sandler

Consultant: Jim Sherman
Head Baseball Coach
University of Delaware

BEARPORT
PUBLISHING

New York, New York

Credits

Cover and Title Page, © Jessica Rinaldi/Reuters/Corbis; 4, © Jed Jacobsohn/ Getty Images; 5, © REUTERS/Ray Stubblebine; 6, © Guido Cozzi/Atlantide Phototravel/Corbis; 7, © AP Images/Andres Leighton; 8, © Popshots/Omni-Photo Communications, Inc.; 9, © Jim Hughes/New York Daily News; 10, © Tom DiPace/ Sports Illustrated; 11, © George Tiedemann/Sports Illustrated; 12, © REUTERS/Ron Kuntz; 13, © Barry Chin/Boston Globe/Landov; 14, © AP Images/Bill Kostroun; 15, © AP Images/Charles Krupa; 16, © AP Images/Amy Sancetta; 17, © Ezra Shaw/ Getty Images; 18, © REUTERS/Shaun Best; 19, © Brad Mangin/MLB Photos via Getty Images; 20, © Ron Vesely/MLB Photos via Getty Images; 21, © AP Images/Charles Krupa; 22T, © REUTERS/Jessica Rinaldi; 22C, © Jed Jacobsohn/Getty Images; 22B, © AP Images/Kathy Willens.

Publisher: Kenn Goin
Senior Editor: Lisa Wiseman
Creative Director: Spencer Brinker
Design: Stacey May
Photo Researcher: Omni-Photo Communications, Inc.

Library of Congress Cataloging-in-Publication Data

Sandler, Michael, 1965–
 Manny Ramirez and the Boston Red Sox : 2004 World Series / by Michael Sandler ; consultant, Jim Sherman.
     p. cm. — (World Series superstars)
 Includes bibliographical references and index.
 ISBN-13: 978-1-59716-628-7 (library binding)
 ISBN-10: 1-59716-628-6 (library binding)
 1. Ramirez, Manny, 1972—Juvenile literature. 2. Baseball players—Dominican Republic—Biography—Juvenile literature. 3. Boston Red Sox (Baseball team) —Biography—Juvenile literature. I. Sherman, Jim. II. Title.

 GV865.R38S36 2008
 796.357092—dc22
 (B)
                    2007038362

For more information, write to Bearport Publishing Company, Inc., 101 Fifth Avenue, Suite 6R, New York, New York 10003. Printed in the United States of America.

10 9 8 7 6 5 4 3 2

★ Contents ★

Fearless

Would Boston win a World Series at last? After two home wins, the Red Sox held a 2-0 lead in the series against the St. Louis Cardinals.

Still, their fans were nervous. Boston's job was about to get tough. The 2004 World Series was headed to St. Louis. Surely the Cardinals would bounce back at home.

Unlike the fans, Manny Ramirez wasn't scared. The Boston **left fielder** was hitting the ball too well. "When I'm doing things right," said Manny, "I have no fear."

Manny had gotten a hit in every 2004 postseason game.

Fans in Boston's Fenway Park cheer the Red Sox during the 2004 World Series.

The Boston Red Sox hadn't won a World Series in 86 years.

The United States

Manny was born in the **Dominican Republic**. His family moved to New York City in 1985. Manny was 13 years old.

Life in the United States was hard. Manny's mother sewed dresses. His father drove a cab. Together, they barely made enough money to pay the rent. They didn't even have a telephone.

Manny got used to many new things in the United States. So much was different—the people, the weather, the language. However, one thing didn't change. He still loved playing baseball!

Manny was born in Santo Domingo, the largest city in the Dominican Republic. It is also the capital.

Baseball is the most popular sport in the Dominican Republic.

Many **major-league** players, including Albert Pujols and Alex Rodriguez, have Dominican backgrounds.

Practice Makes Perfect

Manny was crazy about baseball. It was all he thought about. He spent hours practicing each day.

He learned to be **patient** at the plate and wait for good pitches. He kept his mind clear and **focused** on the ball.

In high school, he became a star. Players called him "the hitman" because of his skills with the bat. Manny's success didn't surprise his coach. "Manny was the hardest worker I ever had," he said.

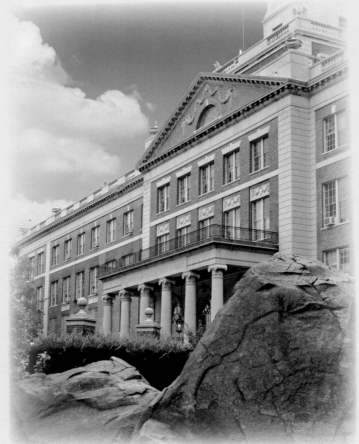

Manny went to George Washington High School in New York City.

Manny slides safely into second base while playing for his high school team.

In his last year of high school, Manny hit .643. That number means he got a hit in almost two out of three trips to the plate.

The Major Leagues

Manny's hard work paid off. In 1991, the Cleveland Indians **drafted** him. Two years later, he made their major-league team.

People loved the way Manny hit the ball. Some, though, thought he was rude because he rarely spoke with reporters.

Manny was not rude, he was just scared. Though he was fearless at the plate, he was nervous in front of a microphone. Speaking English was still hard for him. He didn't want to make mistakes.

When Manny hit his first major-league homer, his friends and family got to see it. The Indians were playing in New York that day.

Manny hitting his first major-league home run

Big Hitter

Soon no one cared how much Manny spoke. He became one of the game's best **sluggers**. Often he batted **cleanup**. His job was to "clean off" the bases by getting a hit and sending the runners home. Manny did his job very well.

In 2000, Manny joined the Red Sox. He chose the team because of its talented players. Manny wanted to win a World Series. Boston, he thought, could do it.

Manny is congratulated by his teammates after hitting a three-run home run for Cleveland.

Manny was excited to join the Boston Red Sox.

In 1999, Manny became the first player in over 60 years to drive home more than 160 runners in one season.

The Red Sox
and the Yankees

The Boston Red Sox had great players. Sadly, they just couldn't win a **title**. Boston's last World Series win was back in 1918.

Often, the New York Yankees knocked them out of the **playoffs**. The Yankees had lots of titles. Their fans loved it when they beat the Red Sox.

When Boston played in Yankee Stadium, the crowd chanted "1918, 1918." New Yorkers liked reminding Boston that they hadn't won a World Series in a long time.

Yankees fans root for their team
during the 2003 playoffs.

Unhappy Red Sox players in the clubhouse after losing to the Yankees in the 2003 playoffs

Even with Manny on the team, the Yankees beat the Red Sox in the 2003 playoffs.

2004

In 2004, Boston again faced New York in the playoffs. When the Yankees won the first three games, no one thought Boston had a chance.

Yet, Manny and the Red Sox battled back. In Game 4, **designated hitter** David Ortiz smacked a game-winning homer. Then Boston took Games 5, 6, and 7!

The Red Sox had beaten the Yankees in four straight games. Unbelievably, they were going to the World Series.

David Ortiz rounding the bases after hitting the game-winning home run in Game 4

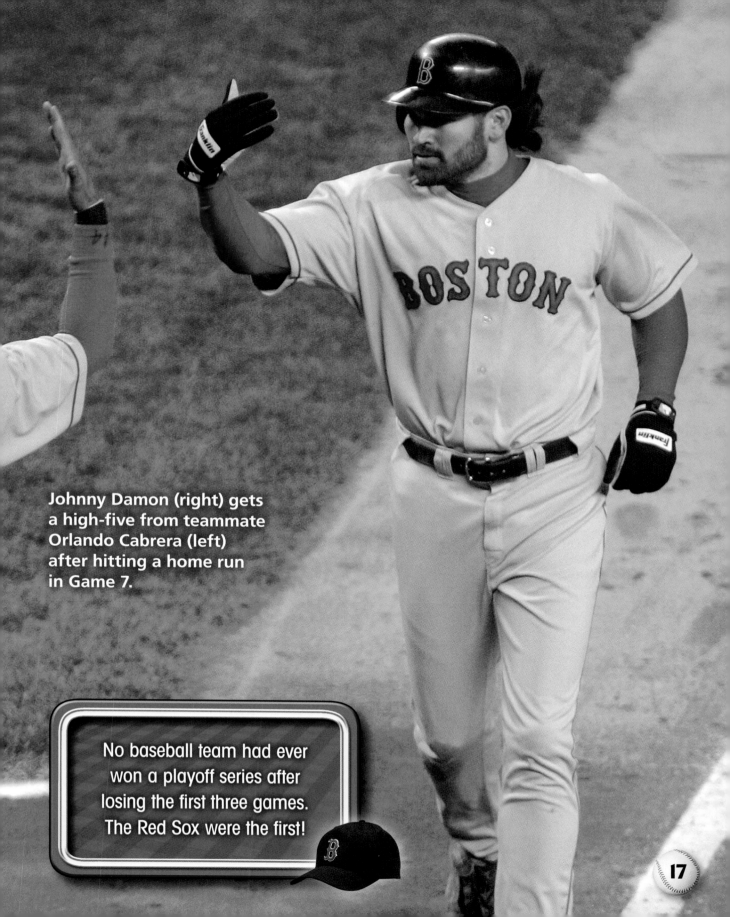

Johnny Damon (right) gets a high-five from teammate Orlando Cabrera (left) after hitting a home run in Game 7.

No baseball team had ever won a playoff series after losing the first three games. The Red Sox were the first!

The Cardinals

Boston's **opponents** in the 2004 World Series were the St. Louis Cardinals, baseball's best hitting team. To win, the Red Sox would need to score a lot of runs.

In Game 1, Manny had three hits and drove in two runs. Boston won, 11-9. In Game 2, pitcher Curt Schilling kept the Cardinals off base. The Red Sox won at home again.

Now Boston led the series, 2-0. However, they still had to win in St. Louis.

Manny's single in the seventh inning of Game 1 drove in a run.

Boston and St. Louis had played each other in two earlier World Series, 1946 and 1967. St. Louis won both times.

Curt Schilling pitched Boston to a 6-2 win in Game 2.

Winners at Last

Manny didn't care where he played, he just wanted to win. In Game 3, he ignored the screaming St. Louis fans. In his first turn at bat, he took a mighty swing. The ball soared over the fence for a homer. Boston never gave up the lead. They now led the series, 3-0.

In Game 4, Boston held the Cardinals scoreless. They won the game and the series. No longer would anyone shout "1918." Manny and the Red Sox were champions!

Manny runs the bases after hitting a home run in the first inning of Game 3.

The Red Sox celebrated their win with a parade through the streets of Boston.

Manny was named Most Valuable Player (MVP) of the 2004 World Series.

★ Key Players ★

Manny, along with some other key players, helped the Boston Red Sox win the 2004 World Series.

Manny Ramirez #24

Left Field

Bats: Right   Throws: Right
Born: 5/30/1972 in Santo Domingo, Dominican Republic
Height: 6'0" (1.83 m)
Weight: 200 pounds (91 kg)

Series Highlights
Had three hits and drove in two runs in Game 1; hit a first inning home run in Game 3

David Ortiz #34

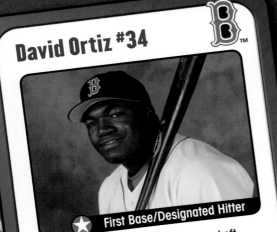

First Base/Designated Hitter

Bats: Left   Throws: Left
Born: 11/18/1975 in Santo Domingo, Dominican Republic
Height: 6'4" (1.93 m)
Weight: 230 pounds (104 kg)

Series Highlight
Drove in four runs in Game 1

Johnny Damon #18

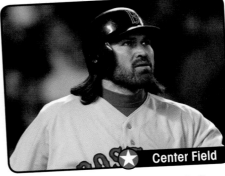

Center Field

Bats: Left   Throws: Left
Born: 11/5/1973 in Fort Riley, Kansas
Height: 6'2" (1.88 m)
Weight: 205 pounds (93 kg)

Series Highlight
Hit a lead-off home run to start Game 4

Glossary

cleanup (KLEEN-uhp) fourth in the batting order

designated hitter (DEZ-ig-*nate*-id HIT-ur) a player named at the start of a game to bat in the pitcher's place without causing the pitcher to be taken out of the game

Dominican Republic (duh-MIN-uh-kin ri-PUHB-lik) a country in the Caribbean

drafted (DRAFT-id) picked to play for a professional team

focused (FOH-kuhsst) concentrated on one thing

left fielder (LEFT FEELD-ur) the player in the left section of the outfield

major league (MAY-jur LEEG) the highest level of professional baseball in the United States, made up of the American League and the National League

opponents (uh-POH-nuhnts) teams or athletes who others play against in a sporting event

patient (PAY-shuhnt) good at putting up with problems or delays

playoffs (PLAY-awfss) games held after the regular season to determine who will play in the World Series

sluggers (SLUHG-urz) players who hit the ball hard and deep into the field

title (TYE-tuhl) the championship; in baseball, it's a World Series win

Bibliography

Edes, Gordon. "Manny Ramirez: Baseball's Best Clutch Hitter." *Baseball Digest* (August 2001).

McGrath, Ben. "Waiting for Manny." *The New Yorker* (April 23, 2007).

Pierce, Charles P. "The Sultan of Swings (and Smiles) Emerges." *Sports Illustrated* (November 10, 2004).

Weinreb, Michael. "A Manny Among Men." *The Sporting News* (June 21, 1999).

Read More

Sandler, Michael. *Baseball: The 2004 Boston Red Sox*. New York: Bearport Publishing (2006).

Vascellaro, Charlie. *Manny Ramirez (Latinos in Baseball)*. Childs, MD: Mitchell Lane (2000).

Learn More Online

To learn more about Manny Ramirez,
the Boston Red Sox, and the World Series, visit
www.bearportpublishing.com/WorldSeriesSuperstars

Index